# Ready
# to Lead?

Marybeth,

Thank you for inspiring
us all to be our best
and take a bigger stand
for the leadership aspirations
of our clients.

Yours,

Alan Price

June 2005

# Ready to Lead?

a story for leaders and their mentors

Alan Price

JOSSEY-BASS
A Wiley Company
www.josseybass.com

Published by Jossey-Bass
A Wiley Imprint
989 Market Street, San Francisco, CA 94103-1741   www.josseybass.com

Jossey-Bass books and products are available through most bookstores.
To contact Jossey-Bass directly call our Customer Care Department within
the U.S. at 800-956-7739, outside the U.S. at 317-572-3986, or fax 317-572-4002.

Jossey-Bass also publishes its books in a variety of electronic formats. Some content
that appears in print may not be available in electronic books.

**Library of Congress Cataloging-in-Publication Data**
Price, Alan.
   Ready to lead? : a story for leaders and their mentors / Alan Price.
      p. cm.
   ISBN 0-7879-6951-6 (alk. paper)
   1. Executive ability—Fiction.  2. Leadership—Fiction.  I. Title.
   PS3616.R524R43   2004
   813'.6—dc22                                    2004001315

Printed in the United States of America

FIRST EDITION
HB Printing          10  9  8  7  6  5  4  3

# CONTENTS

*To Gina*
*Your brilliance ignites my imagination*
*Your love fills me with courage*
*Your smile inspires me to be my greatest*
*Thank you for marrying me*

# Ready
# to Lead?

# CHAPTER 1

# The Performance Evaluation

Mark Gibson paused before entering the conference room. "Relax. Take deep breaths," he told himself. "Annual performance evaluation—piece of cake. OK, not everything went perfectly, but I've worked hard and hit my targets. Revenue and profits are up a bit. Stay focused on the positive and everything will be fine. A raise and promotion might be nice." He opened the door and saw his boss enjoying a view of the Charles River and the Boston skyline.

"Mark, it's good to see you. How are you?"

"Patricia! I'm great. Thanks. How was Denver?"

"Denver is a mess. After this review, I want to talk to you about it."

"Sure. I'd love to help." That seemed like a good sign. Maybe she wanted to send him to Denver to help turn it around.

Patricia Willis closed a thick folder and dropped a pen on the legal pad in front of her. She leveled a friendly but piercing stare at Mark. It felt like she was taking a moment to read his mind. Patricia had an uncanny ability to read people and situations. Seven years of management consulting and ten years as a senior executive had sharpened her gaze to the point where it could be intimidating. "Mark, sit down. I'm going to skip the usual forms and formalities. You already know you're doing well. I'm delighted to report that the firm also knows you're doing well."

"Thank you. This is a great company with great people. I can't believe three years have flown by so quickly."

"Three years really isn't much time. Three years is barely long enough for us to get to know one another—see each other's strengths and preferences. A bad hire can be spotted fairly quickly. But a good

hire takes time to understand. We take the time
to ask questions and look for answers. How will
you perform over time? In what situations will you
succeed or fail? If we push you out of your comfort
zone, how will you function? How will you treat
people when you're under pressure? What types
of people and projects bring out the best in you?
What is your response to winning? We started with
all sorts of questions about you. In your three years
here, we think we have the answers to some of those
questions."

Mark was curious about where this was heading.
Maybe this was going to be like one of those 360-
degree evaluations. Patricia was always candid,
and you could count on her to be brutally honest
without being brutal in the process. Mark remembered a time when Patricia had every reason to
be furious with an analyst who missed a critical
deadline. She'd simply asked, "What can we do
so we can look back at this and laugh?"

Patricia took a sip of water before continuing. "I'm
going to start with some observations you already
know to be true. Mark, you're smart. You have
tremendous talents and potential. You work hard
but still play well with others. Even though you
already know those things about yourself, I want

to start out by acknowledging them as some of your more obvious strengths."

"Thanks, Patricia."

"I also want to share three of your strengths that you may not fully appreciate. First, when you are solving internal production problems, you're a highly creative spendthrift. Rather than throwing money at the problem, you focus your creativity on how to make do with what we already own. Many people now look to you or try to think like you when problems occur on the plant floor.

"Second, you have taken the idea of 'customer focused' to a new level. When you are solving our customers' production problems, you first call their customers to figure out what they really need, why, and by when. By doing that bit of research, you've often helped our customers look good and make a lot more money. And that has helped our customers see us as more than a manufacturer and supplier. They see us as business partners. Both of those strengths are wonderful. They don't teach them in MBA programs, but I think we should integrate them into our new hire orientation series.

"Third, you have a skill that I wish I could develop in others—but for the life of me, I have no idea how to teach it. You have the ability to make mistakes, own up to them, help everybody learn from them, and move on. I know it wasn't easy to tell me that the process you recommended in Rochester was a failure in spite of a million-dollar investment. But Atlanta was about to invest twice as much in the same process. Your report reached them in time to avoid the same mistake. Sometimes the high-lights of a year are the successes. You had several successes. However, the clear high point of your year was how you handled that mistake. It said a lot about your integrity and judgment. Those are some of the reasons why we'd like to keep you on board and continue to invest in you for the long run." Patricia paused and waited for Mark's reaction.

"Wow. Patricia, I don't know what to say. Thanks. I hadn't thought about those situations quite that way. I had a lot of help with each of them, so I don't want to take all the credit. This is just a different level of performance evaluation than I expected. Honestly, I just came in here happy that the bottom-line numbers were good. I thought you would be happy and we'd just talk about next year's goals."

"Yes, goals are an important part of our planning for the future. And I predict that your future here will be bright." Patricia pushed her chair back and stood up. She walked over to the window and looked out at the river. The evening winds were too strong for the scullers to be out on the water. She looked back at Mark, who looked relaxed in spite of his growing anticipation. "There are several paths we might try. One path might involve the mess in Denver. Another might involve our testing center in Malaysia. There are so many possible paths that I'm not going to describe them all right now. Your next assignments, and the overall direction of your next few years, are up to you. You get to make the choice. Your success, however, may depend on some questions about you that still need answers. I can't answer these questions. Only you can answer them."

Mark had the feeling that another shoe was about to drop. Patricia had shared his strengths. Was she going to ask about his weaknesses? Mark reached over to the bowl of mints and unwrapped one. Whatever the question was, he didn't want to answer it with a dry throat.

"Patricia, let me see if I follow you. You're telling me that I'm in the driver's seat. I can control my own destiny here, or I can at least choose from a number of assignments. All I have to do is answer some questions."

"That's right."

"OK, I'm game. Ask away."

Patricia stopped and turned from the window. She looked directly at Mark. "Are you ready to lead?"

# CHAPTER 2

# Are You Ready to Lead?

M ark exhaled, and with no hesitation answered, "Am I ready to lead? Absolutely. One hundred percent. I think I have the experience necessary to step into a leadership position and succeed."

"That's good to hear, and probably what I expected to hear," Patricia said. "I guess it would be helpful if I explained the question. As I said before, your performance has been exceptional. We like you. You are a person of integrity, a hard worker, a smart thinker, and a great manager. However, I believe that you have the potential to be an even greater leader. If you want to take that next step,

then it's my responsibility to help you succeed.
I just want to make certain that we're absolutely
clear before we begin a great deal of work together."

"Well, I'm not totally sure what you're driving at . . .
but I think I am ready to lead. What do I need
to do?"

Patricia sat back down and folded her hands on
the table. "Before we go down that path, perhaps
we should figure out what kind of leadership we're
really looking for." Patricia grabbed her legal pad,
reached across the table, and pushed the pad over
to Mark. "What is your definition of leadership,
Mark? I'd like you to write down your definition
of leadership for me."

Mark stared at the pad then back at Patricia. "Write
my definition of leadership? An awful lot goes into
leadership. This could take awhile."

"That's true. A good definition of leadership might
take some time. But it's worth doing. Leadership
is a highly personal thing and every leader should
have a clear, personal definition of what leadership
means to them. I'll tell you what. You take as much
time as you like. But for heaven's sake, don't make a

big report out of it. Fifty words or less would be good for a first draft. Give me a call when you've got a definition you like."

"OK, I'll give you a call." Mark stood up and stretched as Patricia picked up her folder and walked out of the conference room. Patricia's words seemed reasonable. Leaders should be able to state a personal definition of leadership or a philosophy of leadership.

In the spirit of brainstorming, Mark pulled out a pen out and started thinking. He wrote, "Heroic," "Teamwork," "Communicator," and "Teacher." He wrote, "Leadership is getting results," and "Leadership is helping others achieve amazing things." He soon built a column of words and phrases down the left side of the pad. He underlined the ones he thought were important. He started piecing the words and phrases together. At the end of an hour, he had, "Leadership is a combination of attributes and behaviors. The attributes include courage, honesty, compassion, and drive. The behaviors include setting strategy, motivating others, and holding people accountable for results." It was twenty-nine words. It wasn't snazzy, but it was a start.

Just then, Patricia opened the door and poked her head in. "Are you still working on the definition?"

"Yes. It's kind of fun."

"Would you like some advice?"

"Actually, I would."

"I have a few suggestions. First, if you're not ready after an hour, you should take a break. Get out of this conference room. Do a little research if you want. Sit in a café and think it over. Chat with some friends. Have a fun evening with it. Write a draft that you really like."

Mark said, "See you tomorrow," as Patricia was closing the door. He heard her laugh and say, "Good luck!" He looked at the words on the pad and thought about the suggestions. A little research might not be a bad idea.

He decided to walk to one of the bookstores in Harvard Square before taking the bus home. The young man at the help desk said there was no "leadership" section. He apologized and added, "Depending on what you're looking for, you could try business, politics, self-help, or biography."

Mark started in the business section and scanned the titles. There were stories about leaders, stories by leaders, and academic frameworks for understanding leadership. He thought the shelves bore a striking resemblance to the sports section, where one can read stories by and about athletes as well as sports commentary. He knew from firsthand experience that almost nothing from the sports section would help a reader become a better athlete. Reading never lowered a golf score nor did it make anybody swim faster. Reading about favorite pastimes was fun. Mark found it helped him talk a good game with his friends, but it rarely improved his results. He suspected that the same would be true in the field of leadership. Based on his observations of many organizations of all types, leadership was something most people loved to discuss but do nothing about. Nonetheless, with an eye toward writing his own definition, he purchased a book of leadership quotations.

On the bus ride, a quote from General George S. Patton caught his attention: "Be willing to make decisions. That is the most important quality in a good leader." He wondered why General Patton chose decisiveness. Perhaps it was the military context that made it so important. He thought about several people who were decisive but ineffective leaders. He realized that crafting his personal definition of leadership wasn't going to be easy.

He was home early enough to surprise his wife, Jean, with a cooked dinner. She was delighted. Over grilled chicken and asparagus they shared their stories of the day. Jean described a peaceful resolution to a minor crisis at the youth center she directed. The moral to the story was, "When in doubt, call the parents." Mark described his experience in the conference room. Finally they turned to the definition of leadership.

Jean asked, "Isn't leadership all about vision? Don't you just get a bunch of followers and create a vision?"

Mark sat back. "Vision is important. And I suppose leaders need followers. But what about charisma, honesty, decisiveness, courage, and empathy? Every quote in this book I bought mentions a different attribute that is important for leadership."

Jean put down her glass. "Vision without courage wouldn't get you very far." Jean paused, "You don't suppose this is some kind of psychological assessment—a leadership version of the Rorschach test?"

"I hadn't thought of that. I doubt it. Patricia is more direct than that."

"In that case, why don't you take her advice and sleep on it." They got up to clear the table and clean the kitchen.

His last bit of research for the day was to check the dictionary definition:

> Leadership *n.*
>
> 1. The position or office of a leader.
>
> 2. Capacity or ability to lead.
>
> 3. A group of leaders.

The definition was circular and not particularly helpful. Mark put the dictionary back on the shelf, turned out the light, and went upstairs to get ready for bed.

# CHAPTER 3

# What Is Leadership?

Jean awoke earlier than usual and persuaded Mark to join her for a run. "Come on," she said. "It'll help clear your head so you can create your definition of leadership." The sunrise was gorgeous over Fresh Pond, with the leaves just starting to display their autumn colors. Except for the exchanges of greetings to dog walkers and fellow joggers, they ran in silence, both lost in their own worlds of professional challenges.

In their second lap around the pond, an idea occurred to Mark. He wrote it down over breakfast, shared it with Jean, and left for work earlier than usual. Waiting at the bus stop, he considered his definition, "Leadership is taking people to a higher level of excellence by setting a direction, establishing goals, organizing resources and people, and motivating those people with the strengths of your personal character." It made him smile all the way to the office.

He sat down at his computer and saw an e-mail note from Patricia:

> Mark, congratulations on your first draft.
> Is your definition of leadership different
> from your definition of good management?
> Let's talk about it over lunch. Meet me at
> Henrietta's Table around twelve thirty.
> Get yourself out of the office until then.
> —Patricia

Puzzled and bit irritated, Mark walked out of the office and headed for a nearby park. He thought about what constitutes good management. "How hard can it be to figure this out?" he asked himself. "Jean and I spent two years of our lives getting our MBAs. With all those case studies about managers and leaders, you'd think this would be simple." Many quotes in his book also sounded a lot like good management. It seemed reasonable to him that all the attributes of leaders were also attributes of good managers. Good managers have integrity, communication skills, passion, and all the other personal characteristics too.

Mark sat down near some chess players. He pulled out his own definition and started crossing out words that seemed to overlap with management, "Leadership is ~~taking people to a higher level of excellence by~~ setting a direction, ~~establishing goals, organizing resources and people,~~ and motivating those people with the strength of your personal character." All he had left was, "Leadership is setting a direction and motivating people with the strength of your personal character." That didn't seem quite right. It was good but not good enough. Something was missing.

He stood up and watched a couple of chess games. The players were strong amateurs. They talked better than they played. He walked back to the bookstore to look up management in a dictionary.

Management *n.*

1. The act, manner, or practice of managing; handling, supervision, or control.

2. The person or persons who control or direct a business or other enterprise.

3. Skill in managing; executive ability.

It wasn't much more helpful, but it did seem control oriented, which felt different from leadership.

Arriving early at the Charles Hotel, Mark walked up the staircase to Henrietta's Table and found Patricia already seated in a group. She waved him over. "Mark, let me introduce you to some good people—Peter and Bram. They are from The Netherlands and came here to discuss a possible license of the quality assurance process we developed in Atlanta. They have an interesting application for it in their Rotterdam factory."

"It's good to meet you. Welcome to Cambridge," said Mark. They shared a few stories before Patricia looked at her watch.

"I'm sorry to cut you off. Our guests are scheduled to fly to Atlanta for a tour of our operations. Let me take them downstairs and put them in a taxi. I'll be right back."

Patricia was gone just long enough for Mark to scan the menu. "How did you know I would come in this morning to read your e-mail?"

"Maybe I didn't know. Maybe if you didn't show for lunch I was planning to have lunch here again tomorrow. But I did have a hunch. Was the leadership-versus-management distinction helpful?"

"It was both helpful and frustrating. My definition is more focused now but it's not quite right."

"That's to be expected. Show me your draft." Patricia read it aloud. "Leadership is setting a direction and motivating people with the strength of your personal character." Patricia looked it over for a bit before asking, "What's not right about it for you?"

"Something is missing. I can't figure out what it is."

"Would you like some advice?"

"Sure. Do you have a better definition of leadership I could borrow?"

"Absolutely not. You see, Mark, the point of this is not to regurgitate the right answer. You know that. This is all about you creating your own personal definition of leadership. If it isn't in your own words then it won't mean anything to you when you need it most. That's why there isn't more leadership in the world. Lots of people do their homework and read all about leadership. But very few take the time to personalize and internalize it. If you don't do that, you end up trying, unsuccessfully, to be like somebody else."

"That makes sense to me." Mark scribbled an idea in his book. Then in a casual tone added, "I want you to know that I appreciate your taking the time to talk this through with me."

Patricia smiled with delight. "It's absolutely my pleasure. However, you should know that I'm coaching you with a specific opportunity in mind. You may recall that I mentioned a problem in Denver."

"I believe you called it a mess."

"Yes. Soon, I want to tell you the details about this Denver mess. For now it's enough to say that the Denver operation presents us with a simple problem. It's losing money. Naturally, that concerns me."

"Is losing money the problem or a symptom of the problem?" He'd learned that question from Patricia and knew it would make her smile again. The answer was always the same.

"Of course it's a symptom, Mr. Smart Guy. I don't want to go into the details right now. You're going to have an opportunity to take a look at this mess and see for yourself what the problem is. But first I'm going to ask you to switch gears for a bit. Let's order lunch and talk about you."

# CHAPTER 4

# Inspiration

Patricia handed her menu back to the waiter, leaned toward Mark, and said, "There's a lot of change going on in the company and in our industry. This is a window of opportunity that you don't want to miss. You said you are ready to lead. I've seen your performance. If you say that you are ready to lead, then I believe you. To be clear, your performance review is over. Now we need to figure out the next steps of your future with us, so we need to dive into some important subjects. Mark, what inspires you? Tell me as many things as you can think of."

"What inspires me? I suppose lots of things leave me feeling inspired. A few times each year I listen to a speech or a sermon that inspires me. I've read stories about people that inspire me. Certain places inspire me, like watching the sunset off Key West or camping at Colchuck Lake in the North Cascades. Paintings, architecture, and music can inspire me. And watching people do incredible things like in the Olympics can be inspirational too. That's all I can think of right now."

Patricia wrinkled her brow a bit. "I'm curious about something. For each of the things that inspire you, how long does the feeling of inspiration last?"

Mark thought for a while. Finally he said, "Sometimes the feeling of inspiration can last for a day or two. Usually it's much less—more like a minute or two."

"I think I get the picture. Are there ways in which inspiration changes your behavior? In other words, are you inspired to take action or do anything differently? Or do you just enjoy the feeling of being inspired?"

"I usually just enjoy the feeling. It's a temporary euphoria. After watching Tiger Woods, I might schedule a round of golf that week. That's about all."

Patricia seemed to be searching Mark's face for extra clues. She took a sip of water. "Let's enjoy our appetizers while I think about how to coach you." Patricia took out a pad of paper and started writing in between bites. As she finished her salad, she said, "I'm looking for something in leaders that's hard to describe and even harder to develop. I have an idea that I want you to try out for a while just to see where it goes."

"That's fine. I think I'm ready to hear it."

"I was thinking about the difference between drive and passion. It may be impossible to quantify the difference but I can tell when I'm driven versus when I'm passionate about something. Do you know what I mean?"

"I know the difference," said Mark. "I've talked about this with Jean. When I'm driven, it feels like a powerful push to accomplish something. It's like the force of my determination pushing me to go ahead. And when I'm passionate, I feel like I'm pulled by the project."

"Excellent. Push versus pull—I like that. We're on the same page. What we need more of are leaders who have drive and passion. Drive can achieve results and impress people. But it's passion that rubs off on other people so that they achieve results."

Mark sat back and said, "That sounds right. But I'm left wondering whether you're saying that I don't have passion."

"Not at all. You have passion and drive. You just aren't very aware of how to make yourself passionate or driven. It just happens for you almost accidentally. If you want to step up to the next level of leadership, there is an exercise using the idea of inspiration that will help you understand how to tap into your passion or drive more intentionally."

Mark laughed. "Let me guess. I need to define the word inspiration."

"That's not a bad idea. But I'll make your life easier and tell you the origin of the word. The Latin word is 'inspirare.' It literally means to breathe life into. So the question, 'What inspires you?' really means 'What breathes life into you?' Isn't that a beautiful image?" Patricia paused because it seemed that Mark wanted to think about his own breathing. She continued, "I want you to do something. You might feel a bit silly doing this but I think it will be worth doing. I want you to think of five people in your life whom you respect. These should be people who know you fairly well. You should write down their names. Do you have five people in mind?"

"Yes. Is it cheating to put you on the list?"

"Unfortunately that is cheating. I can be the sixth if you feel like adding to the list later. What I want you to do is take your list of five people and ask them this simple question: 'Do I inspire you?' Listen to their answers. If they say no, find out why not. If they say yes, find out how. Is the assignment clear?"

"Oh, the assignment is clear enough. Where we're going with this is a bit fuzzy."

"You could use some insights into the ways you might already inspire others. That in turn might help you understand the ways you might ultimately inspire yourself or harness your passion. Of course, you might learn something completely different. Keep your mind open. It's Friday. Why don't you use the weekend to have these conversations? Find me when you're done. I'm going back to the office to talk to some people about you."

# CHAPTER 5

# The Opportunity

"Patricia, this is Mark. Is this a good time to call?"

"Good morning, Mark. This is a fine time to chat. It's eight-thirty here in Denver. Are you done or are you stuck?"

"I'm done," he said. "I talked to Jean about it all weekend. We even played eighteen holes of golf together on Saturday. My swing was lousy but the foliage was incredible. I talked to the other four yesterday. Inspiration is a powerful subject for discussion."

"I'm glad you had time to spend with Jean because I want you to get on a plane. Pack your bags for a week. Not too dressy. It's fairly casual here. Call the office to get your flight info from Pat and head to the airport pronto. Meet me here in Denver. I want you to see the mess I was talking about. There should be a good demonstration of our problem tomorrow morning. If you can get here in time for dinner we can go over your assignment before we get started. Can you do it?"

Mark paused, then said, "Absolutely. That's not a problem."

"Excellent. I'll see you tonight. You know that Japanese grill in the technology park area? Seven o'clock. Oh, and Mark? You might want to bring your golf clubs."

□ □ □

The chef performed his wizardry—slicing, chopping, juggling, and sizzling. Rather than sitting at the grill in a larger group, Mark and Patricia continued their conversation in a corner booth.

"You asked five people. How did it go? What did you learn?"

"Patricia, it was incredible. I felt really silly asking, and they felt a little bit strange because I've never asked a question like that. But once they answered, I learned a tremendous amount about myself."

"Of course that assignment was highly personal. Its purpose was to give you insights into yourself that you couldn't get any other way. You don't need to tell me what people said. However, if you would like to share any of the lessons you learned, I'd be delighted to hear them."

"I want to share them because I have a question at the end of this and I want to know what you think. The first thing I learned was that I do inspire people—at least some people, some of the time. That alone was surprising enough. I never really understood that before. It was difficult to believe. When I asked them how, I was even more amazed by what they said. They saw things in me that I never would have seen. At the end, I had to admit that I was inspired too. The idea of inspiring myself, and the excitement that comes with it, is hard to explain. That leads me to this huge question. What am I supposed to do now that I inspire people?"

"Well you always inspired people. Only now you're aware of it. And you want to know what to do now. You might not realize this, but you are also struggling to answer the question of whether or not you are really ready to lead. True leadership comes with tremendous personal responsibility. The first responsibility is to take ownership of your own inspiration and greatness."

"But isn't it dangerous to walk around with a big head? What if my ego gets out of control from all this greatness?"

Patricia laughed. "Mark, don't worry. There's little danger of that. Last I checked, you're still human. Which means that you'll screw up again sooner or later. With any luck the accompanying humiliation will balance out the inspiration and greatness and restore your sense of humility. The challenge is to own up to it all—the inspiration and the limitations."

"I think I can do that. If I can't, Jean will probably give me a swift kick."

Patricia smiled and stared at Mark for what seemed like a long time before asking, "Are you ready to lead?"

"Yes. I'm ready to lead. And I have to say that this answer feels different from the 'yes' I gave you in Cambridge."

Patricia sipped her water before continuing. "Let me make certain that you understand the executive overview of the Denver operation. When we bought Oxford Industrials two years ago, the Denver plant was part of the deal. They design and manufacture pneumatic and hydraulic machinery for a variety of applications. They also sell services such as repairs and technical support. Customers include 3M, Ford, Goodyear, and Owens Corning. They are regarded as one of the best in the business and they're still losing money. Last year we lost about $5 million. Five million isn't the end of the world, but it's a big warning sign. I would like to see a happy ending to this story."

Mark looked a bit worried. "And what if I don't know anything about pneumatics or hydraulics?"

"I doubt the problem is that the machinery doesn't work." Patricia leaned forward and her tone became serious. "That plant employs 132 people. Fourteen of them, including the management team, are top-notch engineers. What we don't need is another hydraulics specialist. What we do need is you."

Mark thought about the situation for a moment. "Why exactly am I needed?"

"I'm going to let you figure that out for yourself. Here's what we're going to see at 9:30 A.M. One of Oxford's long-time customers, Prometheus Technologies, decided not to renew their contract and went with a competitor. The contract was worth about a million dollars a year. A team of six or seven people is going to meet and try to figure out what went wrong and what they have to do to get the contract back. We are going to watch that meeting and learn what's going on."

"Watch and learn? That sounds too easy. What's the catch?"

"As I said before, I want you to figure out what the problem is and why they need you."

"That's all?"

"There is a chance, if I like your answers, that I'm going to ask if you want to run this team."

"Aha. I see the catch. What happens if I do want to run the team?"

"Then you stay here in Denver for ninety days or until you fix things, whichever comes first."

"Why ninety days? Is something about to happen to Oxford Industrials?"

"No. I've got up to one year to develop your leadership skills to the level we need. After ninety days, we'll start thinking about what we need to do next."

"Let me see if I heard you correctly. Developing me as a leader is the priority—not the contract?"

"That's correct. Any other questions?"

"Yes. You said, 'fix things.' Does that mean get the contract back?"

"I'll leave it to you to figure out what's broken and what needs fixing. You can also tell me when it's fixed."

"What happens if I don't want to run the team?"

"Then we will figure out what challenge is a better fit for you. However when you see tomorrow's meeting, I suspect that you won't want to pass this up."

"I do have one more question."

"Yes?"

"What happens to the Denver operation if I run the team but fail to fix things in ninety days?"

Patricia's eyes sparkled with pride as she thought about the question. She was enjoying the challenge of Mark's development. "Before you drive a car, do you ask yourself what will happen if you crash?"

"No, I guess not." Mark thought for a moment before adding, "But I might have asked that when I first learned to drive."

"Fair enough." Patricia chuckled. "But the sooner you quit thinking about crashing, the sooner you relax and drive well. Let me worry about failure and contingency plans. Your homework for tonight is to wonder what will happen if you succeed."

# CHAPTER 6

# All Seems Fine—
# on the Surface

Mark read the agenda on the conference room white board. "1. Customer Loss Review: What went wrong? How do we get them back? 2. Are we in danger with any other accounts? 3. Plant tour for our guests." Based on the seniority of the people in the room, it was clear that they took either this customer loss or Patricia's presence very seriously. The president, CFO, and VP of Manufacturing sat on one side of the conference table. The sales rep, tech rep, and tech support manager sat with Mark along the other side. Patricia sat at one end of the table. The VP of Sales and Marketing, Peter Scalise, was running the meeting from the other end.

It was a well-run meeting in terms of organization and efficiency. After a brief welcoming of the "guests from Cambridge," Peter called on different people to make reports. Anthony D'Allesandro, the sales rep, reported on the history of the account. After eight years as a loyal customer, Prometheus Tech was facing increased competition, a market slowdown, and a growing debt burden. About six months ago they had a round of layoffs and started renegotiating various vendor contracts in their efforts to cut costs wherever possible. After several rounds of negotiations, Prometheus Tech announced that they were taking their business to a competitor for a savings of 43 percent.

Peter then reported on Oxford's overall pricing strategy and how it benchmarked against the competition. He assured everyone that Oxford was "highly competitive" and that it was impossible for the competition to offer anything comparable at such a discount. He suspected that walking away was a tactic to see if Oxford would further reduce prices. Given the current situation, Peter recommended that Oxford hold the line on pricing and hire four more full-time sales reps in order to increase sales during this slump.

The final report came from Michelle Park, the tech manager, who recommended that the sales reps more aggressively promote the repairs and maintenance contracts. "After all," Michelle reasoned, "Oxford needs to shift its focus from machinery to services during this downturn. Services are more profitable."

Following the reports was a brief discussion. There was general agreement that the answer to "What went wrong?" was Prometheus Tech's cost-cutting approach and the larger economic situation. They reasoned that an approach of patience and periodic visits from Anthony would keep the door open to the possibility of future business. Nobody seemed particularly concerned about losing any further accounts. The final message from the president was to keep prospecting until more business was found.

The meeting ended with a round of hand shaking and side conversations about the Denver Broncos. As people were leaving the room, the VP of Manufacturing, Dr. Rajiv Gupta, offered to lead a tour of the plant. Patricia declined, saying she had to make some phone calls. Mark accepted and put on one of the hard hats that were hanging on the wall.

Dr. Gupta introduced Mark to each workstation operator and designer. He gave a short lecture on the pros and cons of hydraulics versus pneumatics.

He described the quality assurance process in great detail. He was extremely proud of Oxford's track record of worker safety. When Mark asked what he thought about losing the Prometheus Tech contract, Dr. Gupta exuded tremendous confidence. "You must remember," he answered, "that their machinery needs are highly particular to their manufacturing process. It is unlikely that a competitor could meet those needs at a lower price. I am confident that Prometheus Tech will certainly come running back to us as soon as they have tasted the inferior quality of this unnamed competitor. In fact, the contract will be bigger than ever because we will either need to replace the inferior equipment or we will have to perform a larger amount of repairs and maintenance."

After having his picture taken with the Shipping Department, Mark ended his tour and rejoined Patricia at the front desk. They walked to the parking lot together.

"Did you enjoy your tour?" Patricia asked.

"Everyone seemed friendly and hardworking."

"Yes, the people are wonderful. However, I don't want you to be fooled by the VIP treatment you received in there. They put on their best behavior because you represent the parent company. They're worried that you'll fire them all and close the plant. Any thoughts about what the mess might be?"

"Two possible conclusions leap to mind. The first conclusion, the one they seem to embrace, is that everything is fine. It's a bit like the sailboat and charts are perfect but we're waiting for the wind to pick up again. Even though the operation looks impressive, I'm not comfortable with the notion that the only problems are outside the company. The second conclusion is that we're in big trouble and nobody wants to admit it. What if the sailboat is sinking but we're blaming it on the lack of wind?"

"Excellent thoughts, Mark. I know it's tempting to sort it all out right now but let's wait until this evening. Right now, somebody is waiting to see you. Did you bring your golf clubs?"

"Yes. They're in the trunk."

"Good. Get ready to lose to the old man."

"Did you say *the* old man?"

"You heard correctly. Let's get going. He's anxious to see the new leader we're developing."

# CHAPTER 7

# Wisdom

S am Pendleton stepped off the golf cart and reached out to shake Mark's hand. "Mark Gibson. It's been a long time. Patricia's been keeping me informed about what you've been up to lately. Welcome to Colorado."

"Thank you, sir. It's a pleasure to see you again. Do you live in Denver now?" Mark and Jean had had a great conversation with Sam last year at the company Fourth of July picnic.

"No. I flew in this morning so I could play a round of golf with you." Sam grinned at Mark's look of surprise. "Patricia tells me that you *think* you are ready to lead. Is that true?"

"Yes, sir. I'm ready to lead."

"OK then, put your clubs on the cart and hop in. Don't be nervous. Haven't you seen an old man play golf before?"

Mark arranged his clubs and himself in the cart, then said, "You're hardly an old man, sir."

"I see. Tell me what you know about me."

"What I know about you?"

"Yes, that's right. If I'm *the* old man then, that must mean something to you. So tell me what it means. What do you know about me?" Sam started driving from the clubhouse to the first tee.

"I don't think I know all that much beyond the corporate bio. You founded Pendleton Technologies in the early seventies. You rode the PC revolution for all it was worth. The business press called you an idiot for selling the company in 1987. When the market started crashing, people said you were a genius. You started The Pendleton Group in 1991, a holding company with an internal management consultancy that I joined three years ago. That's about it." Mark looked at Sam expecting kudos, and was surprised to see him wincing.

"Oh boy. We've got a problem. What are we going to do about this?"

"Excuse me. I'm not sure I know what you're talking about."

"The problem is that you don't know anything about me. You don't know my favorite color. You don't know my favorite foods, books, or music. You don't know about my family. You don't even know that I was once on the *Tonight Show* with Johnny Carson as a singer with a barbershop quartet. If you want to be an effective leader, a leader who is able to connect with people to get things done, then you need to know *people.* Tell me, when you walked through the plant this morning, did you learn anything about the people who worked there?"

"No, not much. I was focused on the plant operations."

"Yes, that's the problem. If you decide you're ready to lead at Oxford Industrials, your first assignment is simple. Arrange to have another tour of the plant.

And this time, get to know the people. I'll give you some bonus information to get you started. The president, Wes Cooper, and the CFO, Denise Kupfer, went to the same high school—only fifteen years apart. The ridiculous part is that neither of them knows that. Nor do they know that six other employees went to that same high school. Neither of them knows much about the people who work for them. Do you understand where I'm going with this?"

"Yes. I think so. But I'm just wondering if I'm up to the challenge. It seems like a lot to fix in ninety days. Getting to know 132 people might take ninety days by itself."

"Don't worry. It just takes awareness and practice. For example, I know you are happily married to Jean. You are both successful in your careers, which is creating some tension; everyone's wondering if you're going to have children, but nobody dares to ask you about it anymore. How am I doing?"

Mark stopped short, "I'm impressed. I'm also a bit spooked."

"You don't need to be Sherlock Holmes. I didn't need to share my observations for you to feel like

I cared about you. In fact, the opposite approach is probably safer and more effective. You can just start off sharing about yourself in a way that shows respect. Don't copy my style or anyone else's style. Do it your own way. Don't worry. You'll do just fine. Why don't we put Oxford out of our minds for a bit? Let's enjoy the sunshine and some golf." Sam pulled a club out of the bag and started stretching.

"That sounds good to me."

The game wasn't close. Mark had a few good drives but he was no match for Sam's relaxed swing and good putting. Mostly, Mark enjoyed the opportunity to spend time with the company founder. Sam had a youthful energy and appreciation of life that kept them both laughing all afternoon. They returned to the clubhouse to continue the conversation over a cup of tea.

Sam proposed a toast: "To happiness, good fortune, and the occasional birdie!"

"Hear, hear!" Mark replied.

"Mark, while we're waiting for Patricia, I want to share a few more thoughts about Oxford."

"I'm listening."

"I'm not going to kid you on this. If you take on this mess, it's not going to be easy. Sure it's a darn good business problem, but that's not the point. You've got a challenge that should not be under-estimated. The challenge is that you're a fish out of water. You're different from the people you'll be working with. It's a common dynamic that most people fail to fully appreciate or cope with. It is a true test of leadership. Let's face it, when you walked into that plant, everyone saw you as different. You're not from here. You don't look like you're from here. You don't sound like you're from here. You're smart enough that a lot of people are going to be put off by you the moment you start talking. You're the outsider and people are just looking for an excuse to test you. Which means that it's the perfect place for you to develop as a leader."

"Why is that?"

"These days, there's a lot of attention paid to people who can lead themselves effectively. That's all well and good if you like working alone. If you want to change the world you have to be able to lead others. When I talk about others, I'm talking about others who may be quite different from you. The number one leadership challenge of the twenty-first century is diversity. If you can only lead people who look like you, act like you, and think like you, then you aren't the level of leader we need."

"Do you have any advice on how to do that well?"

"I suppose I might. Let me see. I know one trap to avoid and I have a suggestion for how you might get started."

"Whatever you want to share, I want to hear," Mark said, nodding vigorously.

"The trap to avoid is relying too heavily on the notion of leading by example. It doesn't work nearly as well as people think. There are a couple of reasons for this. The first reason seems to be that an example is a highly imperfect form of communication. You might demonstrate how to make the perfect boardroom presentation and your audience might only observe how to dress like an executive. The example by itself might not teach what you want it to teach. Which means that you need to communicate about the example you are setting. But even if you are exceptionally clear a second reason still can trap you. Your example is always going to be wrapped tightly around you. It can be difficult for people to separate you from your example. That can make it more difficult for the people who are not like you to learn from the example. Do you see the trap?"

"Absolutely. But are you saying that leaders don't lead by example?"

"No. Great leaders will always lead by example. But they teach with much more than an example. Leading by example is a flawed and painfully slow method for developing more leaders. It's a bit like saying, 'Follow me around for twenty years and I'll develop you as a leader.' That's an old model that sometimes works, but it's too slow for the leadership demands we face today."

"Interesting. I'm not sure how I'll do that. I'll have to think about it for a while. You said you had a suggestion for how to get started?"

"Yes. Before you start, rework your definition of leadership one more time. It contains a world of assumptions. Once you get in the middle of a problem, it's almost impossible to lift your head out of the mess and revisit those assumptions. Ah! Here comes Patricia. I hope I've been helpful."

"Sam, your advice has already been tremendously useful."

"Any questions for me before I head back to the airport?"

"Two questions. First, what is your definition of leadership? Before I revisit my own definition, I want to ask some other people and get a broader range of ideas."

"Sure, I'll give you my definitions of management and leadership. They're not right or true but they work for me. Patricia, you've heard them before. Management is the illusion that we can make an irrational world rational. Management creates a story to make sense of the past and guide our actions in the present. Leadership is the imagination that makes a rational world inspirational. Leadership creates a story of the future that makes our present actions meaningful.

"What's the second question?"

"What's your favorite color?"

"Good question. Purple."

"Thank you, Sam. Thank you for taking the time to fly here to meet me. Thank you for sharing your advice."

"It was my pleasure, Mark. Good luck to you. Why don't Patricia and I chat on the way to the airport so you can have a chance to talk with your wife before you make a decision?"

"That sounds like a good plan."

Patricia tossed the keys to Mark. "You take the car. I'll ride with Sam. Enjoy some free time. Why don't we meet back at the hotel lobby at eight?"

"See you then."

# CHAPTER 8

# The Connection Between Leadership and Management

Mark drove back to the hotel, took out his cell phone, and called home to Jean. "Hi, sweetie."

"Oh good—I was hoping it was you."

"Why is that?"

"No reason other than I wanted to hear your voice."

"I'm glad to hear your voice too. I'm torn about this Denver assignment. It's an exciting opportunity. Patricia is serious about developing me as a leader.

But it would be a long time away from you. What do you think?"

"It all depends."

"On what?"

"It all depends on who you want to become and what you're willing to do to reach that goal."

"How can I be certain that this is the right assignment to take on?" Mark noticed that his hands were sweating.

"If you need certainty, you're really going to limit yourself as a leader. You've done some due diligence, now follow your instincts."

"There's one critical thing I don't know. This will be an intense assignment. We don't usually spend so much time apart. I don't want to be away from you for ninety days, and I don't know how you feel about this."

"I'll manage just fine. This is a busy time for me at work, anyway. Maybe you can come back for a weekend or I could fly out to Denver. We can work this out. And I love you so much that I'm willing to ship you some more clothes so you won't look pathetic."

"You are amazing. Thank you."

□ □ □

After a while, Mark returned to thinking about Sam Pendleton's advice, and took out a pad of paper. "Leadership," he wrote, "is about helping people understand and believe that they are needed to create changes that advance a greater good."

Mark went down to the lobby a bit early and found Patricia already seated at a table.

"Are you ready to . . . " she paused before saying, "meet?" She smiled and Mark laughed.

"Patricia, before we get started, I want to show you my new definition of leadership. Leadership is about helping people understand and believe that they are needed to create changes that advance a greater good."

"That's a great definition. I really like it. I particularly like the words 'understand and believe' because it recognizes that people have a head and a heart. And great leaders have always connected

at both levels. Would you like to know my definition of leadership?"

"Now would be a great time to hear it."

Patricia picked up a small notebook, flipped through
a few pages, and read aloud. "Leadership is the
miraculous process of creation. There are six steps
in this process. The first step is visualizing something new or different. It can be a new solution, a
new problem, a new perspective, a new direction,
or even a new situation for an existing idea, but
something is new.

"The second step is finding the meaning and
purpose that will compel you and others to make
this new idea a reality. The third step is to understand yourself and what you stand for. If you skip
this step, you'll be blind to your own strengths
and limitations.

"The fourth step is communication and connecting
with other people so they can have the opportunity
to make this vision a reality. This is the step where
I like your language of, 'helping people understand
and believe.' If you do this well you'll break through
the layers of cynicism and resignation, pick up sup-
porters, gather resources and start creating leaders.

One way to do this well is to share all of the first three steps." Patricia turned the page and continued reading.

"The last two steps in this process are really management. But without them leadership is just a pipe dream and the idea will never become reality. The fifth step is organizing and aligning the people and resources toward results. This includes establishing and communicating the strategy and milestones to give everyone a sense of direction and progress toward the goal.

"The sixth step is focusing on results and achieving the goals that we created. To do this well requires relentless attention to the first five steps plus a strong system of accountability."

Mark took the time to write the steps down in his book before asking, "Can't a well-managed organization do great things?"

"The challenge for many well-managed organizations is how to create something new or make strategic changes when they've only developed people to take the last two steps. Which leads to our situation at Oxford Industrials. Do you want this assignment?"

"I still have a lot of questions. I suppose the answers will come when I get into the middle of it. I want this assignment."

"Wonderful. I want to follow up on something you said earlier. You weren't sure if Oxford was a good sailboat waiting for the wind to pick up—or a sinking sailboat."

"Yes. That's it exactly." Mark's pen was poised to write. "Right now I'm not sure which it is."

"If you had to make a guess?"

"Based on my limited observation, it feels like a sinking ship."

"Interesting. What makes you lean toward sinking ship?"

"Three things. The first is that nobody at Oxford seems to think the problem is serious. The second is that everyone points outside the company to explain the possible causes. When you combine those two reasons, it leads to a third factor: nobody seems interested in making a strategy or plan to deal with the problem."

"Excellent. Do you see why I thought Oxford might need you rather than another engineer?"

"Yes, I just hope you're right."

"Just to consider the alternative, what if it turns out to be a sailboat in need of a strong wind? Is ninety days a reasonable wait to see if the wind picks up?"

Mark considered this for a moment. "I don't know. From what I saw this morning, the Oxford team seemed ready to wait years before getting concerned."

"That's my impression too. I can tell you from a holding company's perspective, that's not a good sign. Sam Pendleton is a patient man if he has good reasons to be patient. If we think Oxford is doing everything right but needs more time to weather a short-term situation, I have no problem making that recommendation. But given the three factors you mentioned, I think Sam is being very patient to wait ninety days."

"Any advice for me as I start out?"

"If this is a long-term problem and the ship is sinking, I have a few thoughts for you. Long-term problems almost always have the same two root causes. They either result from some fundamentally incorrect assumption that is producing a failing strategy, or they fail the six steps of leadership, particularly step six—accountability."

"Accountability. I have the feeling that you're going to ask me to start firing people."

"Absolutely not. Accountability isn't just about firing people. Lack of accountability in an organization often points to a lack of integrity. People don't say what they will do and they don't do what they say. When the lack of results is discovered, they often try to shift the blame and avoid the consequences. Firing is but one of many possible consequences.

"If the cause is a flawed assumption or set of assumptions, that's a tough challenge for a leader. First you have to uncover the assumptions, which isn't easy when people don't want to say them or they are long forgotten. The assumptions may have made sense at the time the strategy was formed, but were never reexamined or updated as circumstances changed. Second, you need to clarify the new assumptions for a new strategy. You could be right or wrong, the market will ultimately decide."

"What kind of a strategist is Wes, the president?"

"I'll leave that assessment up to you. He's a good man and I think that you can work well together." Patricia looked at her watch and grimaced. "If you don't mind, I'd like to call someone in Singapore before they go into a lunch meeting."

"Go ahead. I've got some work to do myself."

"Don't stay up too late. You've got a big day ahead of you."

□ □ □

Mark went up to his room and hooked up his computer to check his e-mail. After reading through many messages and responding to a few, he opened the message from his wife:

> Mark,
>
> We all reach the point where we dream of packing our bags, walking to the shore, and setting sail for new worlds. But few of us actually set sail.
>
> Many get lost in the dream and never take action. Many pack, unpack, and repack their

bags, but never walk to the shore. Many walk to the shore, enjoy the breeze and the view, only to walk back home. Many step onto the boat, load it with provisions, check the maps and instruments, but never pull up the anchor. Many set sail but only go out far enough to look back at the land from a new view.

A few sail off and break free of the land. They go with the deeper currents, follow the stars that call them, and reach new worlds. Let us set sail for new worlds. Let us reach them together.

You have all my love.

—Jean

Mark smiled. He walked to the window and thought about how lucky he was to find Jean. He looked up at the moon and wondered whether Jean might be looking at it too. Then he tried to get some sleep.

# CHAPTER 9

# Through the Customer's Eyes

W es Cooper, president of Oxford Industrials, greeted Mark as he entered the building. "I spoke with Patricia this morning. She said that you'd be joining us for a while. Welcome to Oxford."

"Thank you, Wes. I appreciate the welcome."

"Just let me know what you need and you'll get it. I've asked Peter Scalise to arrange any senior executive meetings you may need today. There will be an all-company gathering at ten o'clock tomorrow morning to announce and introduce you."

"Oh. Is there any chance we can do the senior executive meetings tomorrow?"

"Sure, just tell Peter. What do you have planned for today?"

"What if I told you that I have an idea for getting Prometheus back as a customer?"

"I'd say that would be a good reason to wait a day for those meetings. Let me walk you over to Peter's office so he can hear this."

They walked down a hallway lined with pictures of company picnics.

"Wes, what do you love most about this company?"

"The people. We have the greatest people. It's like a family."

They turned the corner next to a small conference room and stopped at Peter's office. "Mark, I need to take a look at something on the plant floor. Peter will arrange for anything you need."

Mark knocked on the door. Peter shouted, "Come in." Mark pushed the door open and walked in just as Peter was hanging up the phone. "Mark! Welcome. I understand that you have a lot to do and not much time. Here's what I thought we could arrange today. There's a Sales and Marketing meeting at 11 A.M. to start strategizing on the customer side. We could do a 2:30 P.M. meeting with Manufacturing to review suggestions for reducing inefficiencies. I've arranged an all-company announcement to introduce you at 10 A.M. tomorrow."

"Peter, can I interrupt for a moment?"

"Absolutely."

"That's a great schedule and I really appreciate your arranging it on such short notice."

"But?" Peter asked with a smile.

"I was hoping to talk with folks at Prometheus as soon as possible. If they have any free time today, then that's my first priority."

"Good thinking. I'm not certain, but we can probably arrange a conference call this afternoon."

"Meeting in person would be better, don't you think?"

"Oh. Prometheus headquarters is in Hickory Hills, Illinois. That's just outside of Chicago."

"Good. It's possible to get there right after lunch. Care to join me for a little field trip?"

"Sure," Peter said with a minimum of confidence.

□ □ □

In spite of a driving rainstorm, they were able to land at O'Hare Airport and make it to the Prometheus headquarters. The building looked like an airplane hangar that had been converted to a factory. A tall man in a suit walked toward them as soon as they stepped in the door. "Hello Peter. It's been a long time."

"Too long, I'm afraid."

"And you must be Mark Gibson. I'm Jeff Begley, chief operating officer here at Prometheus."

"It's a pleasure to meet you, Jeff. Thanks for seeing us on such short notice."

"My uncle is sorry that he can't be here for this meeting. This was quite sudden and he is at a trade show in St. Louis. He sends his greetings. What brings you all the way out here?"

"I don't know how much Peter explained on the phone."

"Not much, really."

"Well it's easy to start this story at the beginning. I'm with Oxford's parent company, The Pendleton Group. Officially, I was assigned to Oxford just this morning. My first priority is to talk with critical customers and understand their perspective. What is Oxford doing right? Where have we gone wrong? What can we do better? Any insights and history you can share would be very helpful."

"I'm happy to share my perspective, though I could have told you everything over the phone. But since you made the trip, there's something you might as well see. Follow me." As they walked through the maze of assembly workstations, Jeff spoke loudly to be heard above the noise. "Prometheus makes medical devices that allow patients a fuller range of motion and physical capacity. About twenty-five years ago, my uncle designed and built light-weight but sturdy wheelchairs. About ten years ago, we added power, robotics, and hydraulics and introduced a few new products like hydraulic lifts that could be installed in vans and buses. That's when we started contracting with Oxford." Jeff grabbed a binder from a metal shelf and opened it to show a photograph.

"I want you to see this picture. This mini school bus has the first wheelchair lift we ever sold. Oxford worked with us on the hydraulics. That original lift is still in service ten years later and it works great. Now I want to show you something else. This corner of the building is our repair shop. That hydraulic lift on the floor, the one that is partially disassembled, has failed repeatedly. It has been a maintenance nightmare. Guess how old it is."

Mark said with obvious candor, "I have no idea. Eight or nine years?"

"Try eleven months. Of course it's covered under our warranty. We'll fix and reinstall it as fast as possible. But it's costing us time and money every minute that it sits here instead of being in use. I'll give you three guesses who is the target of my aggravation."

"Oxford."

"You got it. So I called our Oxford account rep, Anthony, and gave him an earful about quality manufacturing and customer satisfaction. Can you guess his response?"

"Hmmm. He either wants to sell you a newer, more expensive design or a services contract to take care of the repairs."

"Congratulations. You're batting a thousand. That's not bad for your first day with the company. Is there anything else I can help you understand about our perspective?"

"Yes. If the quality issue were addressed, is Oxford's pricing really out of line?"

"Somewhat. You're about 10 or 15 percent over the competition. Given our financial pressures, we would still like to see your prices come down a bit."

"Jeff, I'm committed to fixing whatever may be wrong at Oxford. If I succeed, is it too late to win back your business?"

"My uncle taught me never to say 'never.' However, it seems highly unlikely given our current situation."

"I really appreciate your honest and direct feedback. A picture really is worth a thousand words and I'm glad we made the trip. I can see why you are so annoyed with us in spite of some good history working together. Jeff, I have to ask you for a personal favor. I know we've just met today, and it's my first day with Oxford, but I just have to ask."

"What is it?"

"I need some time to fix things at Oxford and then I want to come back here and try to win back your business. How much time can you give me to make things right?"

"My instinct is to say that you've got until tomorrow morning."

"I can't do it by tomorrow morning."

"I'll tell you what. If you rush someone over here to fix this lift for me, at no charge, I'll give you a month."

"You've got a deal. Thank you. If you'll excuse us, Peter and I have some work to do back in Denver."

Mark and Peter buckled themselves in the taxi and headed back to O'Hare Airport, both lost in thought. Peter was the first to speak. "Thank you," he said.

"For what?" Mark seemed genuinely puzzled.

"For taking me with you on this trip."

"I'm glad you could join me. I think it was important for you to be here."

"I agree. Can I give you a little background on why this was more important than you may know?"

"Go ahead." Mark turned in the seat to give Peter his full attention.

"I came to Oxford three years ago. I've been on many sales trips trying to get new customers. I've never met with an existing customer."

Mark stared at Peter. "What stopped you?"

"Company policy."

"There's a company policy against visiting existing customers?" Mark could not hide his astonishment.

"Officially, no. Unofficially, yes. I was hired because sales had fallen flat and Oxford was financially squeezed. There wasn't any money to do much marketing. I was supposed to focus the sales force on landing new customers. That's all Wes wanted from us. All the incentive structures were aligned with the goal of new business. I suggested that we needed to go back to our old customers, but Wes wouldn't hear of it. He was desperate for growth. He thought that new customers were critical to rapid growth. New orders were in the pipeline, but it was too little too late. We couldn't save the company."

"Wes must have been upset to lose the company he started."

"In a strange way he seemed almost relieved. We were running out of cash and facing the possibility of layoffs. Wes was never going to fire a member of his own family. Wes thought Sam's infusion of cash would keep Oxford afloat long enough for the growth to kick in."

"Did you believe that growth would save Oxford?"

"No. Nobody believed it. But we all believed in Wes, so we kept trying. I've never seen people work so hard. In hindsight it was clearly futile."

"Why wasn't Wes more concerned about losing Prometheus?"

"I'm not sure. Maybe it's because he's been right so many times in the past. There's a legend that Oxford almost ran out of money in '76. During a lightning storm one Wednesday evening, the comptroller told Wes that they couldn't meet Friday's payroll. Wes wasn't angry. He went out to the factory floor and turned off all the machines. When the workers gathered around, Wes asked for a long moment of silence. Then everyone went back to work. The next morning a big order came in and Oxford was saved. I don't know if the legend's entirely true, but it kept folks working hard through some tough times."

"That's quite a legend. What was different this time around? Wes must have been able to hold out longer before selling."

"Oxford is much bigger now. One new order, even a big order, would never be enough to save it. I think trust made the sale go smoothly. Wes trusted Sam to look after his family."

"What do you think needs to be done now?"

"If it's all right with you, I'd like to visit a few more of our important customers."

"That sounds good to me. Go wherever you need. I wish I could go with you, but I should at least spend my second day on the job in the office. How quickly can you do those meetings and be back at Oxford for a strategy session?"

"With any luck I can visit four cities in two days. Will that work for you?"

"I'll make it work. Before you set up your road trip, would you mind setting up one meeting for me?"

"Name it."

"I'd like to have a conversation with Wes at ten o'clock tonight."

"No problem." The rest of the drive they were on their cell phones making arrangements.

# CHAPTER 10

# The Difference Between Leadership and Management

"Patricia, this is Mark."

"Hey, how is your first day going?"

"It's been very interesting."

"I'll bet it has. It's eight P.M. now. Does this call mean you've got it all figured out already?"

"Hardly!" Mark laughed.

"Tell me what you've learned so far."

"I flew to Chicago with Peter Scalise today. We met with Prometheus."

"Starting with the customer. Good choice. I like it. How did it go?"

"It looks like quality may have fallen off at Oxford. The original designs work reliably, but at least one recent model seems to need a lot of maintenance and repairs."

"Is that all?"

"I think quality is the secondary problem. The primary problem is that Oxford lost touch with a major customer. Prometheus used to think of Oxford almost like a business partner. Now they see Oxford as an unreliable vendor that only calls to squeeze more money out of them."

"Yes, that is a problem. How will you fix it?"

"I'm not sure yet. I could use some advice. There's an all-company meeting where I'll be introduced to Oxford. It might be a good opportunity to get something started quickly. I'm trying to put my thoughts together about what I want to say. Later tonight I'll meet with Wes Cooper to discuss it. Do you have any advice for what I should say?"

"I think you might say how proud you are to be a part of Oxford and that you are looking forward to getting to know people."

"Definitely. Also, I thought it would be good to mention something about Oxford's history."

"That's a nice touch. You might say a few words about yourself."

"Good. Then what?"

"Then nothing. That's it."

"That's it? Patricia, this feels like an important moment. I've only got ninety days here and I don't want to waste any time getting the word out."

"Really? What word is that?"

"That we're going to have to make some changes. That we're going to have to focus more on our customers if we want to stay in business. We need a sense of urgency. That's the word I need to communicate as soon as possible. What do you think?"

"I think you're trying too hard and you're just going to make people upset."

"What?"

"Don't get me wrong. Everything you just said makes sense, I just don't think tomorrow's meeting is the time and place to say it."

"Why not?"

"First of all, they've probably heard it all before. No matter how much fire and brimstone you put into the speech, it's only going to add to the layers of cynicism that have already built up. Resistance to change will only increase. Second of all, if they haven't heard it before, you're going to scare people into nonproductive directions. Instead of getting them to work harder, that approach is likely to make them start looking for jobs elsewhere because they'll think Oxford must be sinking. Third of all, it's their first time meeting you. Do you want them to think of you as the wacko from Boston who drops in and rants about changing everything? I suspect there has to be a better way to introduce yourself."

"When you describe it that way, it doesn't sound very good. But that's what I would usually do with my team if I thought change needed to happen."

"True. But this is a different situation. Your team knows you already. Oxford doesn't know you.

Your team knows they can count on you. Oxford doesn't know anything about you yet. They'll think you are a lunatic. At least there's a good side to this story."

"Oh? What's the good side?"

"You asked for advice before you did anything foolish."

"Gee, thanks."

"Seriously, that's a very positive start on your leadership journey. Moving from manager to leader is a big shift and it isn't easy. We all make mistakes along the way, occasionally big mistakes. Mistakes are an unavoidable part of the job. The best leaders do two things regularly—they listen to advice before big moves and they listen to advice after mistakes happen."

"All right. I hear you. Thanks. I think I can handle the all-company meeting tomorrow. But I'm not sure how I should solve this problem."

"I'm not sure how to solve the problem either. Even if I did know how, it wouldn't do your development any good to give you the solution.

Whatever you do, I hope you'll try to solve this like a leader instead of like a manager."

"Do I need to go back to the definitions?"

"Not now. I've only got a couple of minutes before my check-in with Sam Pendleton. Let me give you a few ideas and you can go back to your definitions later. As a manager facing a quality problem you would use typical manager tools to fix it. You would implement some form of quality control throughout the production process. You would restructure the organization and the production line to make quality the top priority. You would make quality a major factor in performance evaluations and you would be relentless in rooting out every cause of production defects. You would create financial incentives to reward perfection. Everything from raw materials to shipping would be reinvented. How am I doing?"

"That sounds about right."

"As a manager facing a customer focus problem you would again use typical manager tools to fix that. You would do some form of customer account planning, check your product pricing strategy, and play around with quotas and bonuses to align the incentives to the behavior you want. You would wrestle with the timeless question of how to raise revenues without hurting profitability. You might even try some creative ways to involve the customer in your design process. Am I still on track?"

"Yes. I just have this feeling that you're about to say that all those ideas—ideas I spent a lot of my life learning—are all wrong."

"Absolutely not. They're all good ideas that produce results. They are important tools in the manager's tool kit. They may be exactly what Oxford needs. But before you jump in and start thinking like a manager, I want you to consider what it might be like to think and act like a leader."

"And what would that difference be?"

"Take a look. That's where your definition will come in handy. Mark, I need to go. It's time for my chat with Sam. I'll talk to you soon."

# CHAPTER 11

# Focus on the Mission

The Oxford parking lot was almost empty at night. Mark leaned back against his rental car, looked up at the stars, and thought about the situation. He glanced at his watch. "Jean's probably asleep," he thought.

Mark's cell phone rang and he answered it. "Hello, Mark here."

"Sam Pendleton here. How are you doing, Mark?

"As Patricia probably told you, I'm in the middle of a good challenge. Do you have any advice for what I should do at Oxford?"

"When I was in the Army, we learned to focus on the mission. What's your mission?"

"Figure out why Oxford is losing money and do something about it."

"That's right. It's a good mission—simple and clear. Do you know what I think?"

"No, what?"

"I think you might be one of the few people at Oxford with a clear understanding of his mission. I saw people working hard, but I don't think they had any idea about their mission. Get everyone focused on the mission. That's where I'd start if I were you."

"I appreciate the advice."

"Do you want some advice on your conversation with Wes?"

"I'll take all the advice you're giving."

"Wes is a very smart guy. He's very proud and extremely polite. Which means that he doesn't think he needs you around. He doesn't want you around.

He might even be furious with you. But he'll never tell you that. You're there because I need you there and Wes doesn't have a choice. That's a strange situation but you can use it to your advantage."

"Great," Mark said with sarcasm. "How do I do that?"

"Remember that Wes has surrounded himself with smart people who don't push him very hard. You might just have to push him—gently but firmly— to see what he's really capable of."

"I think I can do something like that."

"That would help Wes tremendously. Good luck with the conversation tonight and the big meeting tomorrow."

"Thanks, Sam."

# CHAPTER 12

# A Problem at the Top

The office door was open. Mark looked in to see Wes standing and leaning over a desk full of large papers. "Knock, knock," Mark announced.

"Good. Come in. Close the door," Wes said without looking up from the papers. "I think we may be up to something big. It's very exciting."

Mark closed the door and walked toward the desk. "Tell me about it."

"In our heart of hearts, Oxford is a great engineering company. We engineer solutions to meet a particular set of human needs. We enhance people's mobility, range of motion, and functionality through hydraulics, pneumatics, and robotics. I see a new growth area where our work will succeed: the home office. Furniture stores, office supply stores, and Internet suppliers have grown tremendously to meet the needs of these telecommuters. But Oxford hasn't done anything for the home office. We've been so focused on helping people get out and about that we overlooked the opportunity to fully enable people in their home offices. When I think about how much we can boost someone's productivity, not to mention self-confidence, I can't help but get excited. Take a look at these drawings. These are some designs of a true twenty-first-century home office.

"I've got five of our best engineers working on this. We should have a presentation ready for Sam Pendleton in a few weeks or so. Tell me what you think. I'd like your honest opinion."

"Let me take a closer look at this." Mark's mind was racing, and he wanted more time to organize his thoughts. He pretended to study the drawings for a while, shuffling from one drawing to the next and occasionally saying, "Very interesting." It was difficult to follow the schematics. More troubling was his difficulty in following the business strategy. Had Wes talked to customers to know if there was a real demand for this? How much investment would be required to bring this to market? What kind of financial return did Wes expect? Wouldn't another product line only increase the existing quality issues? Why didn't Wes talk to Sam before putting five top engineers on this project?

The more Mark thought about it, the more he wondered if Wes was Oxford's problem. If Wes is the problem, how should Mark solve it? Traditional management theory would state that Oxford needed a new president immediately. But there was something about Wes that Mark didn't want to discard. Wes had passion. Passion by itself is never enough, but it's a good place to start.

Mark had a hunch what to do. "Wes, I'm not an engineer but this home office concept looks very interesting. Are you sure you want to hear my honest feedback?"

"Yes. Level with me."

"I'm concerned that your presentation to Sam Pendleton is headed in a direction that will push him to say no."

"Really?"

"Really."

"Is it because he has some other strategy in mind for us?"

"Not at all."

"Is it because he doesn't want to invest more money in Oxford?"

"That's not it, either. I think I can explain better if you'll help me understand a few things about the broader context."

"Sure." Wes sat down, looking a bit puzzled.

Mark sat down next to Wes and asked, "What are your priorities for Oxford?"

"My priorities are simple: treat everyone like they were my own family and build a company that engineers products to enable people. Those have been my priorities since I started Oxford twenty-seven years ago."

"Excellent. That helps me connect a few dots."

"Like what?"

"I think I can connect your priorities, your passion, your focus, and the direction of Oxford. They're totally consistent. You love people and you love engineering. It shows and I'll bet that everyone respects that about you."

"Thank you. That's what I've always been about."

"How do you handle the rest of the company as it grows—the nonengineering parts of the business?"

"I find good people and delegate."

"I see. I think I can connect a few more dots."

"Is there a problem? Are my people letting me down?"

"Yes, there is a problem. I'm not sure that your people are letting you down. However, I have a growing suspicion that you, without realizing it, may be letting your people down."

"How is that?"

"First, you don't know that there is a problem."

"What's the problem? I know we've lost money. For the good of the company I followed the advice to sell Oxford to Sam Pendleton. I knew Sam had the deep pockets to ride out this rough patch while we develop new products. Have you seen another problem?"

"Oxford has at least one problem. Every business has problems. Whenever you solve one problem, some new problem pops up. A lot of managers get frustrated by never-ending problems, but it's a part of the nature of organizations. Fortunately, there is a flip side to constant problems. Every business has new opportunities to see or create. Whenever you seize an opportunity, more opportunities pop up.

"Our challenge as leaders is to face them both: the opportunities and the problems. Many focus on just one. I've seen many presidents who were great at spotting and solving problems but could not create and seize opportunities. That's not your style. You seem to prefer the other side of the coin. You have a passion for creating and seizing opportunities, but you are reluctant to face problems. Am I wrong?"

"Isn't that just the difference between pessimism and optimism? Given the choice, I'd rather be optimistic."

"Not exactly. In fact I think that it's a false choice between problems and opportunities. We need to choose them both because that's the reality of business. When I ask people to be realistic, I'm asking them to face up to both. Wes, I haven't seen you in action long enough to know the details of your style and its impact on Oxford. But it wouldn't surprise me if your reluctance to face the problems was somehow responsible for your having to sell Oxford to Sam Pendleton."

Wes's face grew stern. It was hard to read his expression. Mark started to worry that he had pushed a little too far. After a few moments, Wes took a deep breath. He leaned back and said, "There might be a grain or two of truth in what you're saying. But the company is sold. What's done is done. What should I do now?"

Mark decided to follow his hunch to its logical conclusion and asked, "Are you ready to lead?"

# CHAPTER 13

# Sparks Fly

Abruptly, Wes leaned forward and pointed at Mark. "Perhaps we've had some kind of misunderstanding, but I seem to recall that I founded this company."

"I didn't mean to—"

"Hold on. I've been willing to give you a lot of slack. I was willing to trust you because I trusted Sam. But you've got a lot of nerve asking me if I'm ready to lead. Didn't you hear me talking about going after a new and important market segment? Day after day I do nothing but lead this family. Now that we're struggling, I'm asking you what to do. I don't appreciate getting questions in response to my questions—least of all questions about whether I'm ready to lead."

"Wes. You're right. We've had a misunderstanding."

"Then you're going to answer my question?"

"Yes, I do have some suggestions for what you should do. But my suggestions only work if you answer yes to two questions. I believe that you're ready to lead. So you've answered yes to the first question."

There was a long pause before Wes asked, "What's the second question?"

"Are you ready to reexamine your definition of leadership?"

# CHAPTER 14

# A Time for Reflection

"Good morning, Jean."

"Hey! I'm glad you called. How was your first day?"

"I think it went well. We'll see. Did you have a board meeting last night?"

"Yes. They liked my presentation and they voted to go ahead with the capital campaign."

"Fantastic. That's excellent news. How do you feel about it?"

"I feel great. All that hard work getting ready has paid off, and now we have the true hard work of running the campaign. At the end of this, our children's shelter will grow from a capacity of ten to a capacity of forty. That's what makes it feel so good. It's a long way off, but it feels good now. Do you know what I mean?"

"I know exactly what you mean. I feel good just hearing about it through you. I'm proud of you."

"Thanks. That means a lot. Now, are you going to tell me what's happening out there or do I have to play twenty questions?"

"I don't have a ton of time. I need to check in with Patricia and then head in. So I'll give you the highlights. It's definitely a leadership challenge. I have the feeling that a lot of changes need to happen. But I don't have a handle on what the changes need to be. My whole body wants to get involved in the production line and solve this problem as quickly as possible."

"Is that what you're going to do?"

"Oh no. I'm resisting that urge."

"Good. You're not an engineer, you know."

"I know. Besides, there's an equally important problem on the customer relationship side. Most important, solving the problems by myself doesn't fit with my definition of leadership. I think I need to help create the drive for them to solve the problems on their own. If the company gets focused on this, then it becomes a matter of helping people overcome any obstacles that pop up."

"That sounds reasonable. But there is one tendency you may not have accounted for."

"What is it?"

"Do you remember that time when you tried to prove that the stock market was the pinnacle of economic inefficiency because most investors had no idea what they were buying?"

"Yes."

"Try not to come across like such a smart-ass today."

"Thanks," Mark chuckled. "I'll remember that."

"I love you."

"I love you more."

"We'll see about that."

Mark put down the phone, looked out the window of his hotel room, and stared at the Rocky Mountains. Before long, his thoughts returned to work. "I really don't have a handle on what I'm going to do. Oxford has grown a lot over the years. It's grown to a size that causes a lot of companies to hiccup or stumble. Just when it's strong, smart, and experienced you'd think Oxford would do things that it always dreamed about doing. Instead it seems to be bogged down or going backward. What can we do? Maybe all we need is to recapture some of what made Oxford great in the first place. Maybe we need to borrow some ideas from other companies to help move forward again. Maybe Oxford got so good specializing in different functions that people forgot how to work together toward one goal. How would a leader approach this situation?" After a few more minutes of thinking, he flipped the phone open and started dialing.

"Good morning, Mark."

"Hi, Patricia. Do you have a minute?"

"Sure. Go ahead."

"I think I'm clear about a couple of leadership ideas. I realize that leadership is a very personal thing. People connect with the leader. So I can't duplicate someone else's style. I need to be my authentic self."

"So far, so good."

"Idea number two is to re-ignite their natural passion and drive for excellence. People want excellence. People want to be the best. Oxford's strength is that they've built a team that feels like a family. We need the family to focus on excellence and winning."

"Also good. You might want to think about something broader than excellence. People want a lot of things. People might want relationships, community, a sense of meaning, or a connection to spirituality. It's hard to know unless you really know the individual."

"Patricia, you're right as usual. If you don't mind, I think I'll start with a focus on excellence. As I get to know people, I'll work on those broader goals."

"That sounds reasonable to me."

"That's all for now. Wish me luck."

"You don't need luck. But good luck anyway."

# CHAPTER 15

# Energizing the Company for Excellence

At 10 A.M., Wes Cooper addressed the all-company meeting. "Good morning, everyone."

More than a hundred people, seated and standing, looked up at the company president.

"Yesterday, I had the pleasure of welcoming Mark Gibson into our Oxford family. This morning I want to introduce him to you and you to him. Mark has been very successful with our parent company, The Pendleton Group, for several years. About three months ago, I asked Sam Pendleton to take a look at Oxford and give us advice to improve our financial picture. You may recall that Sam and Patricia Willis came to visit a few weeks ago. Sam and Patricia agreed to loan us Mark for a while. Mark doesn't have an official title, but it might as well be VP of Everything. I have asked him to look at absolutely everything from business strategy to operations. He's not an engineer, but we won't hold that against him." There were some chuckles around the room. "While he's helping us to get back to profitability, I'm asking you to do whatever you can to support him. Mark and I talked late into the night and it's clear to me that he already has some excellent suggestions of what we might do together. Without further ado, let's have a big Oxford round of applause for Mark."

During the applause, Mark shook Wes's hand and stepped forward.

"Thank you. And thank you, Wes, for those kind words. In the short time that I've been with Oxford, I've been very impressed with the people I've met. I am proud to be a part of this family and I look forward to working hard alongside you. We are a company in a unique position in the industry. We have a chance to be the best at what we do. Not one of the best—*the* best. But that's only a chance and there are no guarantees.

"Wes and I have agreed on the first goal we need to achieve. Together we will develop more goals. The first goal is just to get us started. We will win back the Prometheus account in exactly twenty-eight days. We all need to focus on how to do this.

"The solution to this challenge begins with these plane tickets." Mark held up an airline envelope and pulled out two tickets. "These are for a flight from Denver to Chicago that leaves in four hours and twenty minutes. Prometheus is in Chicago. Sitting on the floor of Prometheus headquarters is a hydraulic lift that we made. For reasons that I will never understand, that lift isn't working. Two members of this family who do know how to fix hydraulics are going to take these tickets, fly to Chicago, spend the night, and knock on Prometheus's front door when the sun rises tomorrow morning. Those two people will fix this lift, make Prometheus happy, and be remembered as the two who began the rescue of the Prometheus account. If you want to be one of these two rescuers, talk to Dr. Rajiv Gupta. He will select the heroes of Oxford. The rest of us will support you with whatever you need to succeed.

"By the way, these are one-way tickets. You get the return tickets when the president of Prometheus calls and says that it's all right for you to leave. While you are in Chicago, you'll be guests of Prometheus's chief operating officer, Jeff Begley. He called Peter Scalise to say that his house has a couple of spare bedrooms and we're welcome to crash there as long as we need. Are there any questions?"

From the right side of the group a man shouted, "I have a question. My name is Howard. If Wes says that you're OK, then you're OK. And it's OK that you're not an engineer. But what exactly are you going to do to help us? I don't know how to support you if I don't know what you're doing."

"Howard, thank you for that question. I'm sure a lot of people are wondering what I'm going to do. I haven't been here long, and I'll probably never know Oxford as well as you do. Right now it's too soon to know how we'll get Prometheus back. But I'm going to work with Wes to figure it out. At the beginning we need your ideas for changes and improvements. In the middle and at the end we'll need your hard work to make those changes and improvements succeed."

A hand shot up from the group. "Yes?" Mark asked. "What's your question?"

"My name is Claudia. If I go out to Chicago to fix this lift, it will be fixed." Several people laughed. "And if you send someone with me who knows how to socialize more politely, we will get Prometheus back." The laughter grew more widespread. "What I want to know is, if we get this done fast, do you want the voodoo doll I made of you?"

The group, including Mark, lost its composure in the laughter. The meeting disbanded slowly as people introduced themselves to Mark and welcomed him to the Oxford family.

# CHAPTER 16

# Resistance to Change

The whiteboard was filled with mathematical equations and diagrams. The walls of the conference room were covered with flip chart paper. Mark had invited all the engineers to an urgent discussion on manufacturing quality, opening the meeting with the story of the two lifts at Prometheus and sharing the customer's perception that quality had declined at Oxford. Mark had stressed the importance of winning back the Prometheus account, then turned the meeting over to Dr. Gupta. That was almost two days ago.

All day and well into the evening the engineers wrestled with quality issues. They brainstormed, divided up the list of problems, and worked in small groups to find solutions. They rarely took breaks other than trips to the factory floor to debate whether a particular change would be effective or too costly. Dr. Gupta ran the meeting efficiently. The group appeared to be making progress toward a comprehensive set of recommendations and budget estimates for successful implementation. Mark stepped out of the room when his phone rang. "Hello."

"Hi. This is Patricia. How are things going?"

"I think they are OK . . . but I'm not totally sure."

"You don't sound so great. What's wrong?"

"I'm in the middle of this quality improvement discussion with all the engineers. In a lot of ways it feels productive. But it keeps getting bogged down. They are starting to look tired and frustrated. I'm not clear about what I should be doing."

"Mark, that's good. I'll let you in on a little secret."

"OK. What's the secret?"

"Instead of doing something, you should probably look for something to stop doing. In fact, everyone might be better off if you figured out what you should stop doing."

"Well, that's an easy one to figure out."

"And your answer is . . . ?"

"I should stop putting myself in the middle of these engineers."

"Exactly. Didn't I tell you that the last thing they need is another engineer?"

"Yes, I remember."

"Let me guess, you couldn't help yourself."

"True," Mark said a bit sheepishly.

"No problem. We all make mistakes. Now you know something about one of your tendencies. Write down the lesson learned and move on."

"Thanks. Any advice for moving on?"

Patricia took her time thinking about what advice to give. "Is there someone other than you who could get in the middle of the engineering issues?"

"Yes. Wes Cooper."

"What is he doing now?"

"I sent him out with Peter to meet with customers. Together they are mending fences and rebuilding relationships. Peter tells me that he's seen a whole new side of Wes, and he likes what he sees."

"That sounds terrific. In spite of the newfound role in sales, can you bring Wes back into engineering?"

"He'll love it. He's in Phoenix so it won't take him long to get back. I wanted Dr. Gupta to have an opportunity to lead the engineering turnaround. But I think he's meeting a lot of resistance at this point. I'll figure out how to tell him that Wes will join the meeting."

"Very good. Don't forget that your call to Wes is critical."

"In what way?"

"You could just call him and ask him to return. That would be your management style. It works. But you need to constantly develop your leadership style."

"I've got it. I'm going to call him now. Bye."

"Bye."

Oxford's founder and president didn't carry a cell phone so Mark called Peter and asked him to put Wes on the line.

"Hello, Mark."

"Wes. How are the meetings going?"

"The meetings are extraordinary. It's been eye-opening. I'm ashamed to admit that I've kept Oxford so distant from its customers for so long."

"As you said yourself, 'What's done is done.' The issue is how to create something better."

"Precisely."

"Wes, help me understand something."

"What is it?"

"Something about our conversation energized and refocused you. You switched fairly quickly from the mind-set of a project engineer back to company leader. I stayed focused on the action planning and I never asked you what caused the shift. Do you remember what made the difference for you?"

"I don't remember what you said exactly. But I do remember suddenly realizing that my dream was at risk and that I had drifted off from my core values. You helped me see that I wasn't treating my customers as family. In fact, I realized that I had lost touch with the Oxford family. Oxford has grown and I never took the time to connect with all the new people."

"Have you had any realizations while visiting the customers?"

"Quality is a problem. Peter told me before, but I didn't listen. I was buried in the process of trying to develop new products. It's another way that I drifted off from my core values. Oxford can't enable and empower people by giving them machinery that breaks down all the time."

"It's exciting to hear someone rediscover their mission."

"Thanks for hitting me between the eyes. How is the engineer team meeting going? Have they figured out how to solve the quality problems?"

"It's not going so well right now. It started well, but the resistance to change started to build this afternoon. Dr. Gupta is doing a fine job, but it needs a leader who has the passion to overcome a lot of obstacles. Do you have any recommendations?"

"Tell them I'll be there at eight in the morning."

# CHAPTER 17

# Mentoring

"Good morning! Are you nervous?" Patricia asked as she walked onto the Oxford factory floor and stood next to Mark.

"More than a little. What time is it?" Mark leaned over the railing and put his head in his hands. He was visibly exhausted.

"Ten A.M. What time will Prometheus be here?"

"Two thirty."

"Inviting them here to inspect the redesigned operation was a stroke of brilliance."

"It was Wes's idea."

"Well he didn't get ideas like that before he started listening to you. He's almost a different person. Did you work through the night with the others?"

"Yes."

"How many nights?"

"Four. Or five. I'm not sure."

"Is there anything more you can do?"

"Probably not."

"Then there's not much point in worrying, is there?" Patricia shook her head with a comical attitude.

"Probably not."

"Whoa! Lighten up, Mark. I brought you a great bottle of wine. Why don't we uncork it and raise a toast to the joys of leadership when the glamour wears off and the implementation gets under way."

Mark stared incredulously at Patricia. It was as if he were watching a circus act in the middle of a battlefield. "I've really lost all perspective on this, haven't I?"

"Without a doubt you have completely lost all perspective. You're just paying the price of setting an incredibly high standard and sticking with a ridiculously short time line. At least you've won the respect of the whole Oxford family. I can't believe how much has changed in the twenty-seven days you've been here. They can't believe it either." Patricia gestured at the frenzied pace of final adjustments happening in every corner of the plant. "As I said in your performance review, one of your strengths is taking customer service to a new level. But this time you did it with leadership. That's very different from using management or personal initiative to improve customer service. I hope you realize that you've made a difference no matter what Prometheus says today."

"Not in my book. We win if we win back the account."

"You may not be a natural-born leader but you are definitely driven. I'll give you that."

"Thanks, I guess."

"OK, Mr. Sour Grapes. Moping time is over. Follow me." They walked down the hall and into an empty office. Patricia shut the door and continued. "I know you're tired. I've got a few things I want to discuss with you and this is the only time available. I fly to San Francisco this afternoon. Can you cheer up and focus for a bit?"

"I'll do my best."

"Good. First, I have a suspicion that you've changed your leadership definition. Am I right? Once reality set in, did you update your definition?"

"Yes. I had to."

"Tell me about it."

"I kept tripping on the first step of your definition, 'visualizing something new.'"

"Why was that a problem?"

"Sometimes it makes sense to visualize something new and innovative. Other times may call for different leadership goals."

"Such as?"

"Business survival. The business may need to adapt in order to survive, but that didn't feel like creating a new thing. Also, you told me that sometimes leadership is a matter of not doing something. That helped me think about leadership to shut down a division or project that should have been shut down a long time ago."

"OK. I like this. So what's your current definition?"

"Leadership is the unleashing of human passion toward a goal. And management is the organizing of skills and resources toward a goal."

"Those definitions are fantastic. If you forget them after your much-needed sleep, I'll be sure to remind you. I said before that you're not a natural-born leader. I want to be clear that the comment was a compliment."

"In what way?"

"Without a doubt most leaders are made, not born. For the most part it doesn't matter how a leader comes into being. Good leadership is good leadership, whatever the source. Where the two diverge is in the area of leadership development. Natural-born leaders typically have no idea how to develop leadership in others. It came naturally for them so they don't have an appreciation for the development process. When natural-born leaders are in charge, there is a risk that they will churn through a whole organization trying to find leaders rather than develop leaders."

"Patricia, that's all very interesting but I'm having a hard time understanding why you need to tell me this now." Mark started stretching and pacing to get his blood flowing.

"When I see you so exhausted, I know you need this information. If you're working this hard under time pressure, you're probably not doing any leadership development. It's a downward spiral. If you don't mentor other leaders, then you have to work harder under more time pressure. Do you see the problem?"

"I see it and I'm living it. I get the message. I can see that I was so busy leading that I wasn't developing more leaders. I spent time developing Wes and Peter, but I didn't look at the middle and lower levels at all."

"That's common. It's a cultural assumption. Most people define leaders as 'people who have followers.' The lead-follow model isn't wrong. It's just limiting. Do you remember when the win-lose model for negotiations was the only model?"

"Yes. That was very limiting; a zero-sum game."

"You see? Then along came win-win and value creation models and a world of new options came with them. The same opportunity is available with leadership. The leadership development process will grow in strategic importance. In the struggle for competitive advantage, organizations will evolve from lead-follow to lead-lead."

"All right. I'm with you. But can you tell me more about the process of developing leaders? I could use some practical suggestions that work even when a person's tired beyond tired and stressed beyond stressed."

"Strictly speaking, I don't develop leaders. I can't develop leadership in you or anyone else. My goal as a mentor was to give you the opportunity and support to develop yourself to be a leader. My model for leadership development is fairly simple, but I adapt it to the needs and goals of each individual leader."

"Let me guess the first step. A person has to choose to be a leader?"

"Very good. That's why asking 'Are you ready to lead?' is so important. Do you want to guess the second step?"

Mark started to look a bit more energized. He felt like he was trying to play a quiz show game. "Sure. It has to do with defining leadership for yourself."

"Right again! I have found that studying other people's definitions of leadership produces a lot of leadership discussion but very little leadership action. It's important that each leader develop a personal definition and act according to a personal standard. Care to guess at the next step?"

"Creating a vision?"

"Only if that's part of the definition. It was a trick question. The next steps depend on the individual definition."

"Only two steps?"

"There is a third step after they've learned to lead. They need to help others develop themselves as leaders."

"Are the leadership definitions all that different from one another?"

"Of course there are common themes. Leaders usually want to connect with other people at some level of mission, purpose, or greater meaning. And most leaders want to produce results of some kind. But a subtle difference in the choice of words can yield powerful differences in action."

Mark continued his pacing and thinking. "I like it. I like the simplicity in the structure. I like the adaptability to the individual. I'm ready to try it. Is there anything else I should know?"

Patricia thought for a while. "When you're mentoring, you need to create a challenge that takes them out of their comfort zone. But at the same time you have to create a safety net so that they'll try new things. There's no magic formula. Just be very aware of both."

"OK. I have four people in mind that I'd like to mentor with this model. Help me get started."

Patricia paused and walked over to stand in front of Mark. "I'm sorry to tell you this, but you need to finish up your work at Oxford. You can develop more leaders in your next position. I'll gladly help you then."

"But it's only been twenty-seven days," Mark protested.

"I know. This is sudden. You've done a remarkable job and you'd like to stick around and see it through. You don't need to fly tonight. Celebrate what will certainly be a victory with Prometheus. Get some rest. Take a couple of days for a smooth transition out so people will have a chance to say good-bye. Then I'll see you again back in Cambridge."

# CHAPTER 18

# The Leadership Development Paradox

"Mark! This is Sam Pendleton."

"Happy birthday, Sam."

"How did you know it's my birthday? And where on earth did you find a putter with a purple grip?"

"Can't leaders keep a few secrets?"

"I suppose so. Thank you for the wonderful gift."

"You're welcome."

"I understand that you've done a great job at Oxford. It's amazing that Prometheus doubled their order with Oxford after that visit."

"It's been my honor."

"Do you know what impressed me most?"

"I have no idea."

"You changed the company without throwing away the people. That's a rare feat. Most folks in your position would start firing people. Heads would start rolling from the top on down. Any fool can fire people. It takes a lot of courage to develop and motivate them instead. Congratulations."

"Thank you."

"There's something I want you to do."

"What's that?"

"I want you to write down what you learned from the experience. Take some time to reflect on what you did well and what you might do differently in your next assignment."

"I'll do that."

"I want you to add another page or two on leadership. Write it as if you were passing along advice to

a new leader. Include your current leadership definition, of course."

"OK. That will be a good exercise for me. I have a
few thoughts that I ought to put down on paper."

"Excellent. When you're done writing, I want you
to actually hand that advice to a new leader."

"But Sam, I've only been a leader for a little while.
I'm not sure that my advice will be all that helpful
to someone else."

"Mark, I completely understand your resistance.
You can be a leader your whole life and never feel
like an expert. The so-called leadership experts
usually just study leadership; they don't actually
practice it. Many of the best leaders wait until their
careers are over before writing down any advice for
new leaders. Unfortunately that just cheats the next
generation of good advice and cheats themselves out
of becoming greater leaders."

"I'm not sure I follow you."

"It's a leadership development paradox, I guess.
Most people want to wait until they've mastered
leadership before they write down any advice and
share it. But only by writing down their advice,

sharing it, and discussing it can people achieve mastery in leadership. Trust me on this. If you make it a habit now, your growth as a leader will accelerate rapidly."

"OK, Sam. I'll try it."

"Let me know when you do. I want to hear how it went and what you learned from the discussion. Then I'll do the same for you."

"What do you mean?"

"I have a list of leadership tips that I'll share with you after you've shared your advice with a new leader."

"I can't wait. Sam, can I call you back? Jean is trying to reach me."

"Let's talk next week. Give Jean my best."

"I will. Thanks." Mark switched calls. "Hi, sweetie."

"Hi. I love you."

"I love you. I just had an amazing talk with Sam Pendleton, who sends you his regards. Now I get to chat with you. I feel great."

"How would you like to feel even greater?"

"I'll take that."

"Mark Gibson . . . "

"Yes?"

"You're going to be a daddy."

"What? Really?"

"Definitely. Barbara came over and held my hand while I waited for the test to turn pink. We didn't have to wait long."

"Jean that's incredible. This is amazing. I wish I were with you."

"I wish you were here too. There's a lot I want to talk about with you."

"Me too. I've been questioning this whole life-on-the-road plan for a while. I love the work, but I hate being away from you. A baby gives me even more reason to talk about some work-life rebalancing."

"That sounds good. Are you thinking up some new definition of leadership at home?"

"Maybe."

"When can you come home?"

"I'm not sure. I have a few things to wrap up but I'll get a flight as soon as I can."

"Call me as soon as you know. And, Mark?"

"Yes?"

"Don't tell anybody just yet."

"Why not?"

"I want it to be our secret for now."

# CHAPTER 19

# Taking Leadership
# Up a Notch

As Mark walked to the conference room, he felt the same nervousness he'd felt before his performance review a few weeks ago. He had changed a lot in that short time. "Relax. Take deep breaths," he reminded himself as he knocked on the door.

"Come in," Patricia said. "Sit down. It's good to see you back in Cambridge. You're looking well."

"Thank you. It's good to be home."

"I'll bet it is. Time at home is precious in this business. Which leads me to the question of whether you're ready for a new opportunity."

"What's the opportunity?"

"That's up to you."

"Excellent. What are the choices?"

"Mark, are you ready to lead?"

"Yes. I am ready to lead."

"I'm going to challenge you to take your leadership one step higher."

"I accept."

"Great leaders are able to identify or create their own opportunities. It's a skill that takes practice. It's the one aspect of leadership where entrepreneurs have an edge on the rest of us. Entrepreneurs have to identify or create opportunities or they fail. Most of us are never held accountable for seizing opportunities in quite the same way. The Oxford opportunity was handed to you. It was an important experience in your leadership development, but you didn't have to create or identify the opportunity."

"I see the difference."

"I'm challenging you to identify or create your own opportunity."

"How much time do I have?"

"How much time do you need?"

"Hmmm." Mark started pacing the room while he thought. There were so many opportunities within The Pendleton Group. He wondered about whether leadership in a services company looked different from leadership in a manufacturing company. He thought about some of the consulting clients out-side Pendleton. Perhaps a not-for-profit organiza-tion would be a good situation. It was even possible for him to initiate a new acquisition and run that company.

Patricia tried to cover her smile as she watched him. "You look like a kid in a candy store."

"I'm coming to grips with the idea that you've simply asked me what I want, and that I have no answer. I'm going to need a little while to do some soul-searching, some research, and have a long talk with Jean."

"I know how that process works. Take as much time as you need. Say . . . forty-eight hours? I'll be back Thursday morning. You can tell me then." Patricia started toward the door.

Mark looked only slightly panicked, but remembered his questions. "Two bits of information might help me choose wisely."

"What's that?"

"This isn't going to be another ninety-day assignment, is it?"

"Definitely not. That was an opportunity to test you, stretch you, and give you a break to recalibrate. If your first leadership assignment goes on too long, you run the risk of internalizing some bad habits. Now I have a much better sense of how to coach you and develop your leadership potential. I hope you also have a better sense of how to develop yourself as a leader." Patricia stood in the doorway.

"Good. The Oxford assignment was short and focused. But I think I need to experience the realities of leadership that a long-term assignment would help me develop."

"Good thinking. Be careful what you wish for. You had another question?"

"Yes. I was thinking back to the definition of leadership you told me in Denver. It was a systematic, step-by-step definition. It really helped me wrestle with the difference between leadership and management. But the more I thought about it, the more it seemed like someone else's definition. The Patricia I know would have cut to the heart of the issue with fewer words. Am I wrong?"

Patricia smiled. "You know me well. I'm impressed. Yes, that was someone else's definition. That was the first definition I wrote when Sam Pendleton started mentoring me in leadership. I gave you that definition because it breaks down the elements and helps people develop their own definitions. The definition I use today is very different."

"If you don't mind my asking, what is your definition today?"

"Leadership builds a community of purpose. Management builds a community capable of purpose."

After a moment of staring at each other, Patricia stepped out into the hallway. Mark sat down, opened up his journal, and started writing.

# ACKNOWLEDGMENTS

A great number of people have supported the development of this book and its author with patience, wisdom, love, and encouragement. While it is impossible for me to express the depth of my gratitude to each of them, I wish to acknowledge those most directly connected to this creation. In the fall of 1999, the phone call that altered the direction of my career came from John P. Kotter of Harvard Business School. "Would you like to come over to HBS and help me figure out how to unleash millions of leaders for the next century?" How could I say no to that vision? Professor Kotter was forming the Global Leadership Initiative, a team of leadership thinkers and practitioners assembled for one purpose: help HBS develop more and better leaders. I am indebted to HBS and the GLI team for placing in my hands the responsibility of managing and co-leading that team. Direct thanks go to Warren Bennis, David Choi, Gary Hammel, Linda Hill, Spencer Johnson, Douglas MacGregor, Nitin Nohria, Scott Snook, and Ellen Pruyne. Our research and development, discussion and experimentation pushed at the boundaries of leadership, technology, and education. Those ideas, combined with my consulting, coaching, teaching, management, and leadership experience, were the catalyst for this book.

I am fortunate to have friends, clients, and colleagues who have been generous with their time in guiding me through every stage from conception to publication. Tom Ehrenfeld was the angel on my shoulder for the entire two-year journey. Without his help, this book might not have materialized. Spencer Johnson and Don Schmincke also helped demystify the process of becoming an author. I raced through the early drafts with help from Kim Budd, Kristi Budd, Laura Downing, Stefan Einarson, Sheila Heen, Tom Kennedy, Ben Lummis, Will Young, David Pincus, Laura Willis, and Bob Volpe. Ruth Allen, Grace Bartini, Stacey Blake-Beard, Chris Bogden, John Branson, Roy Edelstein, Miriam

Hawley, Steven Kastenberg, John Lemkemeier, William Thompson, and Grant Ward encouraged later drafts. Ellen Pruyne and Jeffrey MacIntyre went the extra mile to dissect the text and the author so that both would tackle the central issues head-on.

Several people warned me about the dangers, frustrations, and difficulties of the publishing process. Thankfully, I was able to sidestep most of the traps. I was fortunate to have a fabulous agent, Daniel Greenberg. His instincts about the book and its audience were always accurate. He taught me that even great chapters should be thrown out if they don't fit with the book as a whole. Susan Williams and her team at Jossey-Bass are the editors and publishers that all authors hope for. From the beginning Susan understood the book's potential. Then she was relentless in making certain that it lived up to that potential.

Mentors come in many forms. At many times in my life, mentors stepped forward and offered their guidance. Don Semenza, Fernando Figueredo, and Gerald Beirne were significant influences in my youth. Through chess, photography, and stock market analysis, they honed my curiosity and gave me glimpses of how to be a renaissance person in a modern age. Richard Smith, my drill sergeant in the Army, instilled in me the confidence to overcome all obstacles. The faculty of Earlham College succeeded in awakening the teacher within me. At Earlham I learned that community, culture, principles, and purpose can all be intentionally and collectively created. Roger Fisher, Bruce Patton, Alan Dershowitz, and Charles Ogletree gave my studies at Harvard Law School a personal passion. They helped me and many others see that law can be used in countless ways to serve and improve society. Irma Tyler-Wood and C. Mark Smith started me down the path of helping organizations wrestle with their most challenging internal dynamics. Carol Beasley coached me to be more coachable so that I could accelerate my development as a leader. Frank Duehay pushed me into community involvement and public service. Reverend Thomas Mikelson taught me that public service, done well, is another form of ministry.

There is a special group of friends I have had the honor of coaching while I was just starting to create a new model for leadership development. Jan Campbell, Elise Ehrlich, Rick Humbolt, Suzy Kratzig, Danielle Mancini, Juan Murray, Kobi Pincus, and Reverend Marta Valentin had the courage to look at their businesses, careers, and lives with me. After remarkably short conversations, you each articulated your dreams and started living them. You showed me that I have a gift for guiding people to discover or rediscover their distinctive, extraordinary purpose.

I am blessed with two families, one through birth and one through marriage, who generate unconditional love on a daily basis throughout the ups and downs of life. Cheryl and Gary are amazing siblings. I am so proud of you. My siblings-in-law, José, Saloua, Renée, Ralston, Danielle, and Khristian are equally tremendous. My parents-in-law, Calvin and Cheryl, kept me focused on reaching the finish line. My parents, Cyril and Doris, would go to the ends of the earth for me. They read every draft with love and an eye for accuracy. I pray that I can be as worthy a parent. My wife, Gina, chose to take on the role of reading the author, but rarely the book. You pushed me to keep writing without being pushy. You gave me space to write without going away. Our two sons, Jackson and Griffin, did what little boys do best—infected me with love, laughter, and a spirit of playfulness. May you never lose that spirit.

A.P.

# THE AUTHOR

ALAN PRICE is president of INSPIRITAS Corpora-
tion (www.inspiritas.com), a consulting and
training firm advancing the practice of leadership
development. He served as director of the Global
Leadership Initiative (GLI) at Harvard Business
School in 2000 and 2001. Working with distin-
guished faculty such as John P. Kotter, Nitin Nohria,
and Warren Bennis, GLI developed world-class
tools and teaching materials.

At the time he was invited to help organize GLI,
Price was COO and CFO of ThoughtBridge, a
consulting firm specializing in negotiation strategy,
labor-management relations, and dispute resolution.

He served as an infantry lieutenant in the U.S. Army National Guard. Price has a J.D. from Harvard Law School and a B.A. in economics from Earlham College.

He invites readers to post their favorite leadership definitions and read others at www.readytolead.net.